Cambodia
Animal Rescue

Rob Waring, *Series Editor*

HEINLE
CENGAGE Learning™

Australia • Brazil • Japan • Korea • Mexico • Singapore • Spain • United Kingdom • United States

Words to Know

This story is set in the country of Cambodia. It happens near the city of Phnom Penh [pnɒm pɛn].

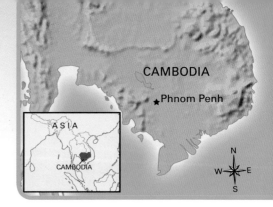

CAMBODIA

★Phnom Penh

ASIA

CAMBODIA

N
W — E
S

(A) Animals in Danger. Here are some animals that you will find in the story. Label the pictures with words from the box.

| bear | crested eagle | elephant | gibbon | tiger |

1. _____

2. _____

3. _____

4. _____

B Animal Rescue Center. Read the paragraph. Then complete the definitions with the correct form of the underlined words.

In the wilderness areas of Cambodia, there are not many people. Because of this, poachers often go there to catch wild animals to eat or to sell. They have killed so many of some types of animals that the animals are now an endangered species. If they don't get help, there will soon be no more of them left! Now there is a special team that rescues these animals and takes them to the Phnom Tamao [pnɒm təmaʊ] Rescue Center. There, a group of volunteers protects and helps the animals. These people don't get any money for their work. They only get the satisfaction of caring for the beautiful animals of Cambodia.

1. An _____ is a living thing which may soon no longer exist because there are so few alive.

2. _____ are people who catch and kill animals illegally.

3. To _____ something is to give it food, water, and all it needs for daily life.

4. A _____ is a person who does a job or offers help without pay.

5. The _____ is a place far away from people that is in a completely natural state.

6. To _____ something is to help it out of a dangerous or unpleasant situation.

5. _____

Dara is a beautiful tiger that loves just lying around and relaxing. She also likes to be touched and talked to. Like many other animals, she really loves to play as well. Unfortunately Dara, and the other animals that live with her at the Phnom Tamao Rescue Center, are all **victims**.[1] They're victims of the illegal poaching of wild animals in Cambodia.

The Phnom Tamao Rescue Center is a stopping point for animals that people have saved from poachers. Once they are ready, many of these animals will be brought back to the wilderness to live in a safer area. But how did these animals get here?

---

[1]**victim:** someone who has suffered the effects of bad treatment, illness, or bad luck

CD 1, Track 03

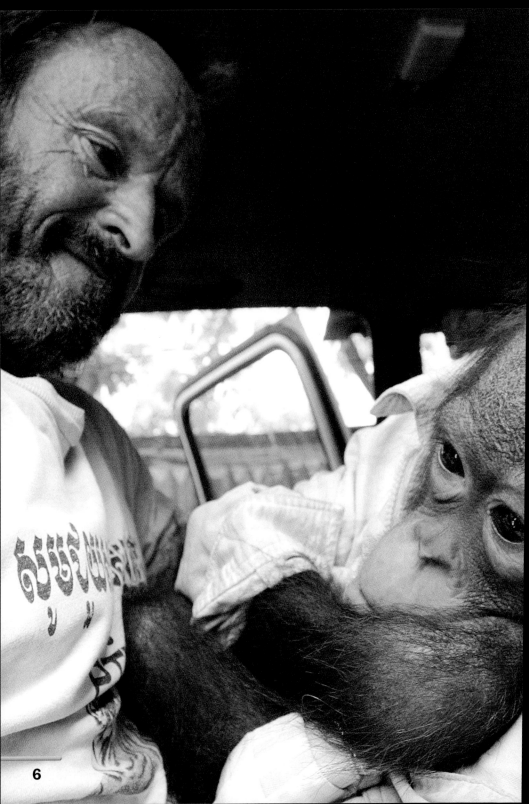

Many of the animals at the Rescue Center were brought there by a special team. The team is called the 'Wilderness Protection **Mobile**[2] Unit,' or the 'M.U.' for short. The job of the M.U. is to drive around the country of Cambodia and rescue animals from poachers. With the support of the leaders of Cambodia, the M.U. is working very hard to stop poaching in Cambodia.

In many cases, these rescued animals can be returned to the wild quickly. But in other cases, the animals need more time or special care. That's when the Phnom Tamao Rescue Center becomes involved.

---

[2]**mobile:** able to go from place to place; traveling

Recently, a pair of crested eagles was rescued. They're going to need a lot of special care before they can be returned to the wilderness. Matt Young works for Wild Aid, which is a U.S. group that **sponsors**[3] the M.U. and the Rescue Center. He talks about what is going to happen to the eagles while he prepares to feed them: "Once we're sure they're nice and healthy again, we can get them out to **Kirirom**[4] and re-release them."

However, caring for wild eagles isn't as easy as one might think. These wild eagles must be 'hand fed,' or given their food from a person's hand. They don't always like this method and Matt has to work hard to get them to eat. He finally succeeds and the birds enjoy their meal. "Did you get that?" he asks the bird playfully. "Fantastic!" he says when the bird eats the food.

---

[3]**sponsor:** give money or help to support an activity, event, or organization
[4]**Kirirom:** [kɪrərɒm] a national park near Phnom Penh; a national park is a protected area for animals

This wild crested eagle must be hand fed.

The crested eagles will probably be released back into the wilderness one day. However, not all animals at the center will be so lucky. Many of the animals that were brought in by the M.U. will need human help forever.

For example, there is a little gibbon at the center that was forced to live in a bird **cage**[5] at a gas station for two years. She's now living at Phnom Tamao and the team is caring for her. They're helping her to become healthy, but they probably won't be able to release her again. The gibbon was always kept by people. It might be hard for her to go back into the wilderness. She might not know how to care for herself. She'll likely be much safer, and happier, at the Rescue Center.

---

[5]**cage:** a structure where animals or birds are kept so that people can look at them

Like the gibbon, Mimi the bear was also someone's pet. How did Mimi get to the center? A volunteer who works for Free the Bears, which sponsors Mimi, explains: "A family bought it for their little daughter, but they only kept her for … I think they said four weeks. And then they realized she was a bit hard to handle—a bit **nippy**[6] and everything—so they just brought her in [to the center]."

Mimi is like the little gibbon in other ways, too. If she were in the wilderness, she probably wouldn't have the skills to survive. She wouldn't be able to find things like food and a safe place to live. The best place for her, too, is clearly the Rescue Center.

---

[6]**nippy:** tending to use the teeth in play; likes to softly bite or 'nip' things

Identify the Main Idea

Skim pages 11 and 12 and answer the questions.

1. Why can't the little gibbon and Mimi the bear be released back into the wild?

2. What do they need?

All the animals at the center have their own stories, even Dara and the other tigers. Unfortunately, there is one thing that many of these wild animals have in common—poachers want them! If many of these beautiful animals, especially the tigers, were not at the Rescue Center, they would be dead. But why do poachers want these animals so badly? Why do they risk hunting them illegally?

The leader of Wild Aid explains what part of the problem is for tigers. She says that poachers can make a lot of money by selling a tiger's body parts illegally. In some Asian countries, certain parts of the tiger are **ground into powder**.[7] This powder is then processed and sold as an expensive **traditional medicine**.[8] People think that taking the product will improve their health. No one knows if this is true, but people should know that it's not good for the tigers!

---

[7] **grind into powder:** make something into very small pieces (a powder) by pressing it between two hard surfaces
[8] **traditional medicine:** medicine that is not approved by doctors that is often based on the beliefs of a country or people

The Phnom Tamao Rescue Center cares for over 800 animals of 86 different types, or species. That's a lot of animals, but they all seem to be healthy and to enjoy being at the center. The tigers get to play before eating, and some animals, like the elephants, even get baths!

Lucky is an elephant that was saved from poachers two years ago. Her friend, little Sima, is a baby elephant who has been at Phnom Tamao for six months. When the animals are relaxing and playing at the center, it's hard to think that they may never return to their wilderness home again. Because they didn't grow up in the wild, they can't survive there. These animals now need to be at the Rescue Center. They need support and help from humans.

All the animals are well cared for at the Phnom Tamao Rescue Center—some even get baths!

A few years ago, Cambodia had about five thousand wild elephants, but now there are just a few hundred. Many animals here, and around the world, are in danger due to illegal poaching. The Phnom Tamao Rescue Center is working hard to help the victims of poaching in Cambodia. It's providing a caring environment for these beautiful animals that can no longer be in the wilderness.

Unfortunately, the bigger problem of illegal poaching is still around. It will be a problem as long as there's a demand for products that are made from these animals. For now, we can only hope that the M.U. can help. Maybe they can stop the poachers from turning more of Cambodia's wild animals into endangered species. Luckily, thanks to Phnom Tamao Rescue Center, the animals that they save will have a safe place to go!

Summarize

Answer the questions. Then, imagine you are a TV or newspaper reporter. Make a short report about this story. Use information from the questions.

1. Why do the animals have to be rescued?

2. Who is helping them?

3. Why are some animals now endangered?

4. What can be done to help stop this?

After You Read

1. In paragraph 2 on page 4, 'they' refers to:
  A. the poachers
  B. the people at the rescue center
  C. tigers like Dara
  D. the animals at the center

2. In paragraph 1 on page 7, the word 'rescue' in the phrase 'rescue animals from poachers' can be replaced by:
  A. stop
  B. organize
  C. help
  D. save

3. How many crested eagles have recently been rescued?
  A. ten
  B. seven
  C. two
  D. twelve

4. Crested eagles don't enjoy _____ hand-fed.
  A. being
  B. having
  C. to
  D. must

5. On page 11, what is the purpose of the second paragraph?
  A. to show an animal that will be released soon
  B. to talk about an animal that currently lives at a gas station
  C. to show an animal who will always live at the center
  D. to explain how the center rescues animals

6. Which of the following is an example of 'human help'?
  A. being fed by humans
  B. living in the wilderness
  C. being a family's pet
  D. being taken by poachers

7. A good heading for page 12 is:
   A. Family Keeps Bear for Four Years
   B. Bear Will Stay at Rescue Center
   C. Bears Make Great Pets
   D. Bear Rescued From Poachers

8. In paragraph 1 on page 15, 'badly' means:
   A. nicely
   B. poorly
   C. little
   D. much

9. According to page 15, why are tigers poached?
   A. because people sell tiger parts
   B. because tiger medicine can save people
   C. because people want tigers as pets
   D. because tigers are beautiful

10. The rescue center has _____ than 800 animals.
    A. over
    B. much
    C. up to
    D. more

11. Which of the following is a danger faced by wild animals in Cambodia?
    A. the rescue center
    B. poachers
    C. other animals
    D. all of the above

12. Why can't some animals return to the wilderness?
    A. because they like people
    B. because they enjoy their life at the center
    C. because they don't know how to survive alone
    D. because they are endangered

These Bears Need Your Help!

DANCING BEARS?

Yes, dancing bears. For hundreds of years, a group of people called the Qalandars has forced wild bears, called sloth bears, to dance. Originally these trained bears only performed in the homes of rich people. This is how the Qalandars earned their money. Today, thousands of these sloth bears perform for the general public on the streets of some cities.

WHY DO DANCING BEARS NEED MY HELP?

The Qalandars buy the sloth bears from poachers. These poachers find the bears in the wilderness, catch them, and sell them. The trainers do not treat the bears well. The sloth bears are kept tied up so they can't walk around. The bears are not trained in a nice, friendly way. Most dancing bears are not very healthy due to the rough treatment they receive.

A Dancing Bear

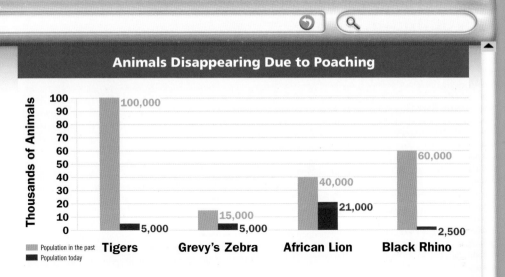

Animals Disappearing Due to Poaching

Tigers: Population in the past 100,000 / Population today 5,000
Grevy's Zebra: Population in the past 15,000 / Population today 5,000
African Lion: Population in the past 40,000 / Population today 21,000
Black Rhino: Population in the past 60,000 / Population today 2,500

HOW DOES 'SAVE THE BEARS' HELP THEM?

We have several key programs that help these poor bears:
- At the Dayalu Rescue Center, rescued bears can live their lives in a safe and comfortable place.
- The Saadaa Animal Hospital provides care for bears that are sick or have been hurt.
- The Khara Training Center helps the Qalandar community to find other ways of making money. There are several successful programs for training people to repair bicycles, to become metal workers, or to start their own small business.

WHAT CAN I DO TO HELP?

Sloth bears are quickly becoming an endangered species. Don't let them join the other disappearing animals in the chart above. We need to act now to save them. If you live near one of our rescue centers, please volunteer your time. Help us to find and care for the rescued bears. If you don't live near a center, contact us directly for more information about ways to help save these beautiful, gentle animals.

CD 1, Track 04

Word Count: 327
Time: _____

23

Vocabulary List

bear (2, 3, 12, 13)

cage (11)

care for (3, 11)

crested eagle (2, 8, 9, 11)

elephant (2, 16, 18)

endangered species (3, 18)

gibbon (2, 11, 12, 13)

grind into powder (15)

mobile (7)

nippy (12)

poach (3, 4, 7, 15, 16, 18)

rescue (3, 4, 7, 8, 11, 12, 15, 16, 17, 18, 19)

sponsor (8, 12)

tiger (2, 4, 15, 16)

traditional medicine (15)

victim (4, 18)

volunteer (3, 12)

wilderness (3, 4, 7, 8, 11, 12, 18)